A New True Book

THE ESKIMO

THE INUIT AND YUPIK PEOPLE

By Alice Osinski

The author would like to thank Linda J. Ellanna, Ph.D., University of Alaska, Juneau, for her assistance.

A hunter searches along the ice for seals.

PHOTO CREDITS

Alaska Pictorial Service:
© Steve McCutcheon—Cover, 2, 4 (top), 7 (right), 14, 16, 17, 19, 22, 24 (2 photos), 25, 26, 29 (left), 30, 31, 34, 35 (4 photos), 36 (top), 39 (top, bottom left), 41 (2 photos), 42 (2 photos), 43 (2 photos), 44 (3 photos), 45

Tom Stack & Associates:
© Caron Pepper—6, 9 (left), 40
© Mark Newman—7 (left), 9 (right), 10, 12 (right)
© Dale Johnson—8
© Rod Allin—11
© Tom Stack—12 (left)
© Byron Crader—32

Alaska Historical Library:
© F.H. Nowell—13, 29 (right)
© C.L. Andrews Collection—20

Root Resources:
© Kenneth W. Fink—21
© Jane P. Downton—36 (bottom), 39 (bottom right)

Roloc Color Slides—33

Len Meents—4 (bottom)

Cover: A snow-covered arctic scene

Library of Congress Cataloging in Publication Data

Osinski, Alice.
The Eskimo.

(A New true book)
Includes index.
Summary: Describes the natural environment and traditional way of life of the Eskimos, contrasting their old customs with the new lifestyle brought by modern civilization.
1. Eskimos—Juvenile literature. [1. Eskimos
I. Title.
E99.E70782 1985 979.8′00497 85-9691
ISBN 0-516-01267-3

Printed in the United States of America.
2 3 4 5 6 7 8 9 10 R 94 93 92 91 90 89 88 87 86

TABLE OF CONTENTS

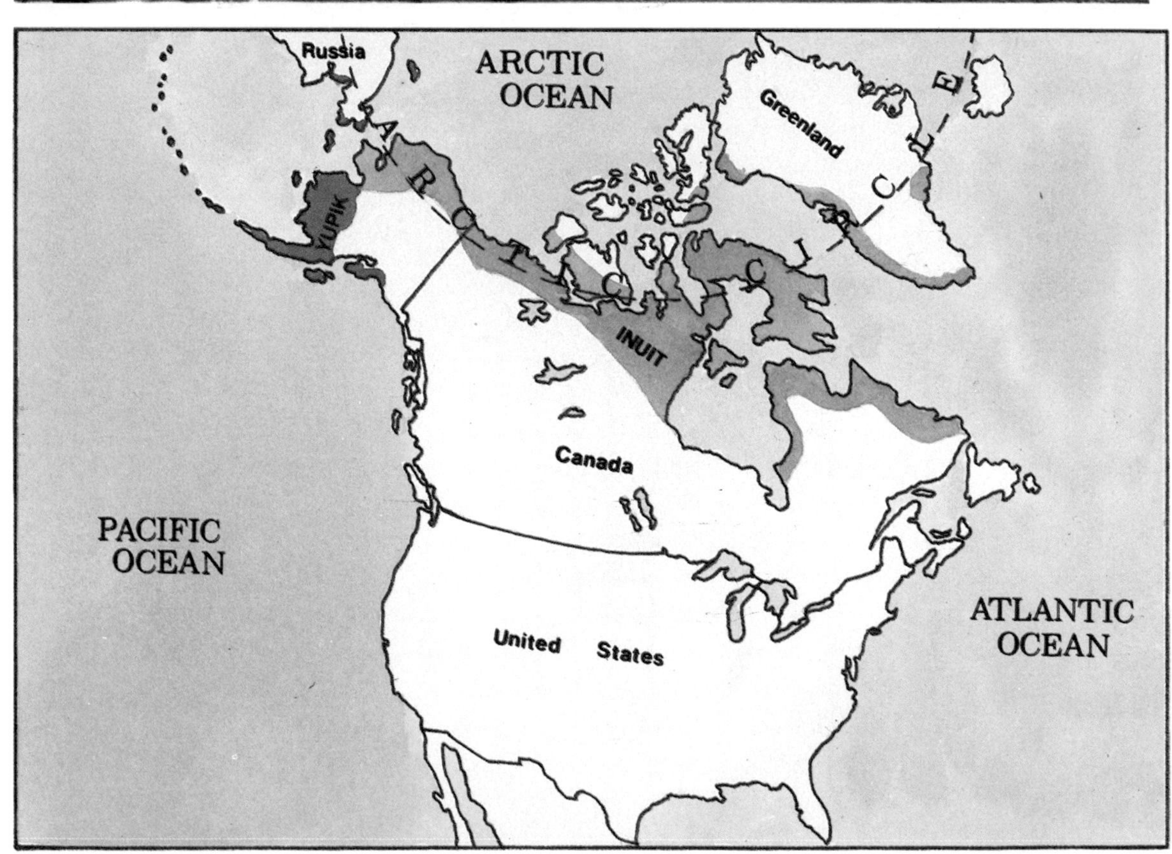

Russia
ARCTIC OCEAN
Greenland
YUPIK
ARCTIC CIRCLE
INUIT
Canada
PACIFIC OCEAN
ATLANTIC OCEAN
United States

PEOPLE OF THE FAR NORTH

At the northern tip of the earth lies a land of snow and ice. It is the arctic. South of the arctic is a region called the subarctic.

Two special groups of people live on this land that stretches from Russia to Greenland, across Alaska and Canada. They call themselves Inuit and Yupiks ("the real people"). We know them as Eskimo.

A LAND OF FROZEN BEAUTY

Inuit and Yupik people live in one of the coldest but most beautiful regions of the world. They have learned to live with the cold—whether on the snow-covered plains in the north, on the grasslands or in the forests of the south,

Snow covers the land most of the year in the arctic, although it snows very little.

or inland from the coast.

For those who live in the arctic, cold is a constant companion. Except for three months of the year, the land remains frozen.

Spring arrives late. Snowfall still occurs in March and April. By May and June the snow melts. For three months the land becomes a swamp of freshly melted streams,

Mouselike lemmings (left) and caribou (above) spend the summer in the arctic.

grass, moss, berries, and wild flowers. Herds of hungry caribou, musk-oxen, and tiny lemmings return to feed off the berries and moss. Many kinds of

Horned puffins (left) live in the arctic waters.
Walrus (right) rest along the shores in summer.

birds come back. The sea is alive with seals, walrus, and whales. Salmon return in spring and summer.

Musk-oxen have curved hooves to help them travel easily.

July and August are the summer months in the arctic. The temperature often does not get warmer than 59 degrees Fahrenheit. By the middle of September light snow begins to fall again.

By October the first heavy snowfalls begin. All living things prepare for the coming winter, when temperatures can fall to 50 degrees below zero.

The arctic fox (below) and the willow ptarmigan (right) each grow a new white coat for winter.

HUNTING FROM SEASON TO SEASON

To survive in the cold climate Inuit and Yupiks learned to live as the animals lived. They dressed in animal skins and followed the animals from season to season.

A hunter harpoons a bearded seal.

They learned to trap, hunt, and gather everything that could be eaten or used.

Most people lived along the coast and hunted seals year-round. In winter and spring they hunted seals on foot. In summer and early fall, seals were hunted from small boats.

Hunting seals in winter took the most patience. Seals live below ice in winter. When they need air, they swim to a breathing hole they have made in the ice. A hunter may wait many hours, or even days, before a seal comes to the hole where he waits. When a seal appears, the hunter has to harpoon the seal before it goes

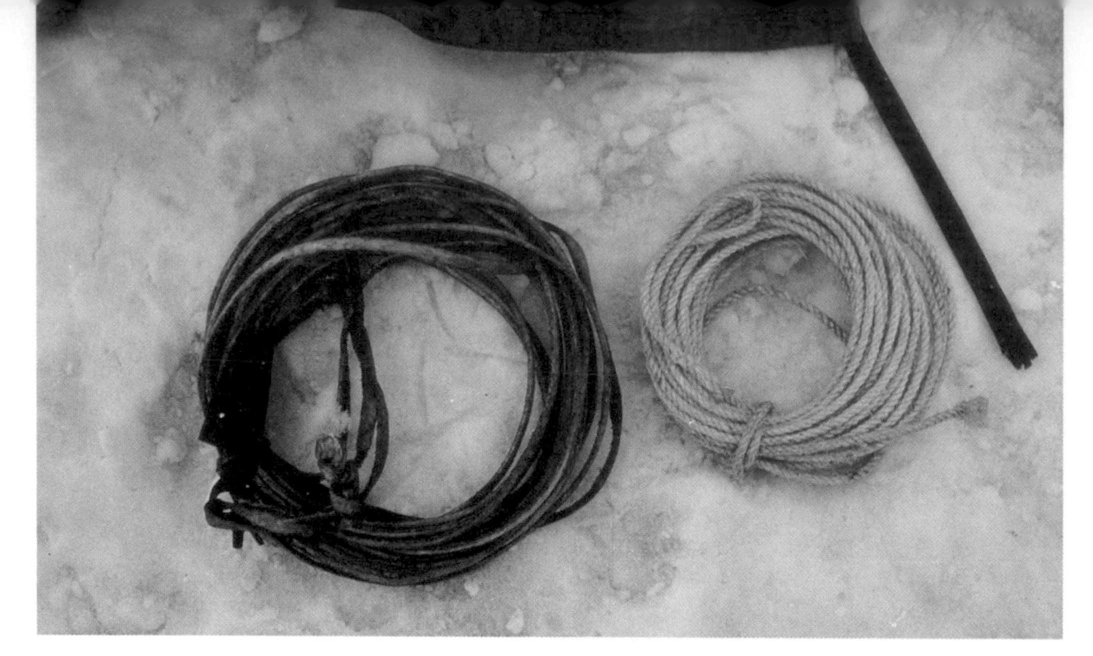

Walrus skin rope (left) is twenty times stronger than regular rope.

below the ice again.

In the past most of what Inuit and Yupiks needed came from the seal, caribou, salmon, and the walrus: meat, clothing, tents, boats, tools, oil for heat, light, and fuel.

A Yupik woman dries salmon for the winter.

Whales were hunted along the coast in spring and summer. People hunted caribou also. They hunted seabirds and collected bird eggs. Along rivers they trapped or netted fish such as salmon, char, and trout.

CROSSING LAND AND SEA

Like all hunters, Inuit and Yupiks traveled year-round to find food. To make travel easier, they built boats and dogsleds.

Dogs carried backpacks during summer hunts and pulled sleds in winter and spring. Sleds were made of bone or wood slats sometimes tied together with animal skin.

Sometimes wood is scarce in the arctic. When driftwood is found, it is often carried long distances.

Today some families still use dog teams for travel. Four to twelve huskies make up a team. The front dog is the lead dog. He listens carefully for directions and then leads the other dogs.

Hunters in kayaks, 1925

Boats were an important means of travel in spring and summer. Two types of boats were used: kayaks and umiaks. The kayak was small. It carried one or two people. It had a wooden frame covered with seal or

A modern kayak

caribou skin. A hunter usually wore a waterproof jacket when riding in a kayak. The jacket was attached to the boat. It sealed the rider in the boat and kept him afloat if the kayak tipped over.

Modern umiaks often have outboard motors.

The umiak was a large, open boat. It could carry more than ten people. It was made of bearded seal or walrus skin stretched and sewn together over a wooden frame. It was used for long trips or to hunt large sea animals.

SUMMER AND WINTER HOMES

Inuit and Yupiks usually did not build permanent homes, except those who lived in Alaska. Instead, they built shelters that could be quickly and easily made. They built houses strong enough to withstand bad weather.

Most families had summer and winter homes.

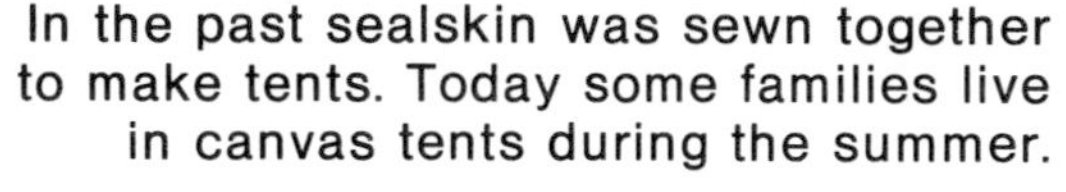

In the past sealskin was sewn together to make tents. Today some families live in canvas tents during the summer.

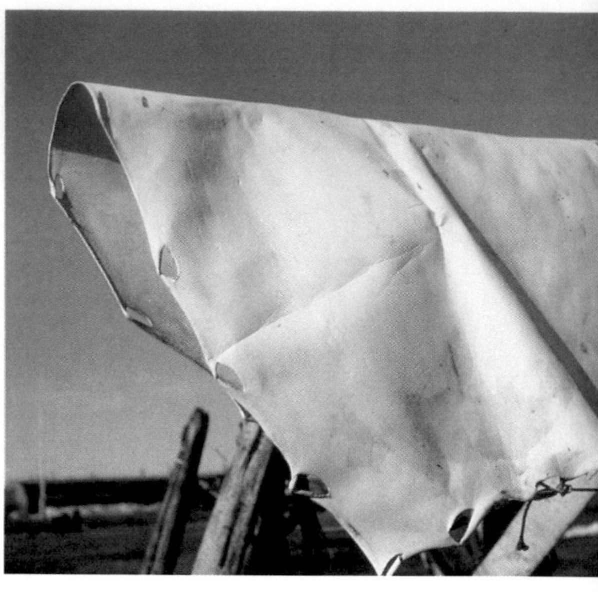

During the summer some people lived in tents. Women made the tents by sewing the skins of caribou or seals together. They stretched the skins over driftwood, whale, seal, or walrus bones.

A sod house

In winter families built sod houses or snow houses called igloos. Sod houses were made of soil and were built partly underground. Often they were used for more than one winter.

Snow houses were made of blocks of hard-packed snow. Usually snow houses were built on ice where hunting was good. Two men, working quickly, could build an igloo in two hours. Sometimes skins, used for the family tent in summer, were hung inside the igloo to help keep out the cold. A lamp, carved from a soft stone called soapstone, was placed in the center of the igloo for warmth and light.

Sometimes several families camped together at winter hunting grounds. They joined igloos together with tunnels so they could visit one another without going outdoors.

KEEPING WARM

Both Inuit and Yupik women made clothing from caribou skin. It was the best kind of animal skin for cold climates. It was warm and light. Skins of seals, polar bears, squirrels, and arctic foxes were used, too.

Everyone wore a hooded jacket called a parka. They also wore pants, socks, mittens, and boots. Tiny skin boots were even put

Caribou skin (left) was dried in the fall. It took almost twelve skins to make a set of winter clothes for an adult.

on dogs' paws to protect them from the sharp ice in spring.

In colder regions people wore two jackets. The inner jacket had fur

Children learned tasks at an early age. Girls were taught to prepare food, make clothing, and care for babies. Boys learned to hunt and to build igloos.

next to the skin for warmth and softness. The outer jacket had fur on the outside. Clothing was loose fitting. It trapped warm air between the body and the cold air outside. A woman's parka had extra

In some areas raincoats are still made from intestines of seals.

room in the back so a baby could be carried against her warm body. In summer people usually wore only a rainproof suit of seal intestine.

Women made all the clothing by hand. Many hours were spent fixing

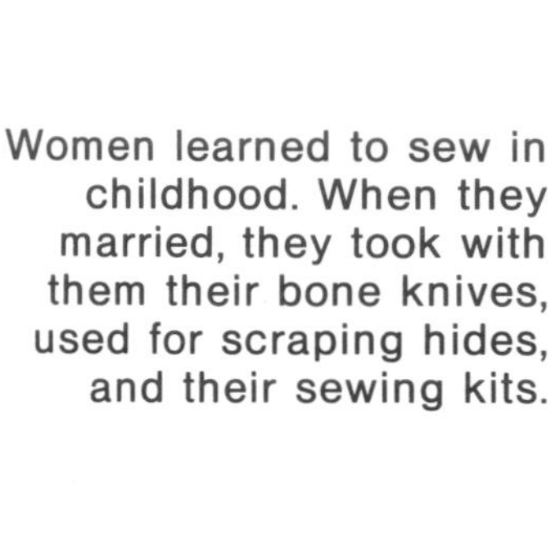
Women learned to sew in childhood. When they married, they took with them their bone knives, used for scraping hides, and their sewing kits.

worn clothes and preparing skins for new clothing. Women took special care of their husbands' clothing. They dried the clothes each night. In the morning, if the men's boots were hard, the women chewed them to soften the hide.

ART AND STORYTELLING

Inuit and Yupik families spent much of the long winter months inside their homes. They made things they would need for hunting and cooking during the year. They also played games and told stories called legends.

Some people made beautiful carvings of the animals they hunted. In Canada most carvings were made from soapstone. In Alaska bone and ivory were used. Carving was a special art. Not just any stone was used. An artist spent time holding a stone and thinking about it before carving it.

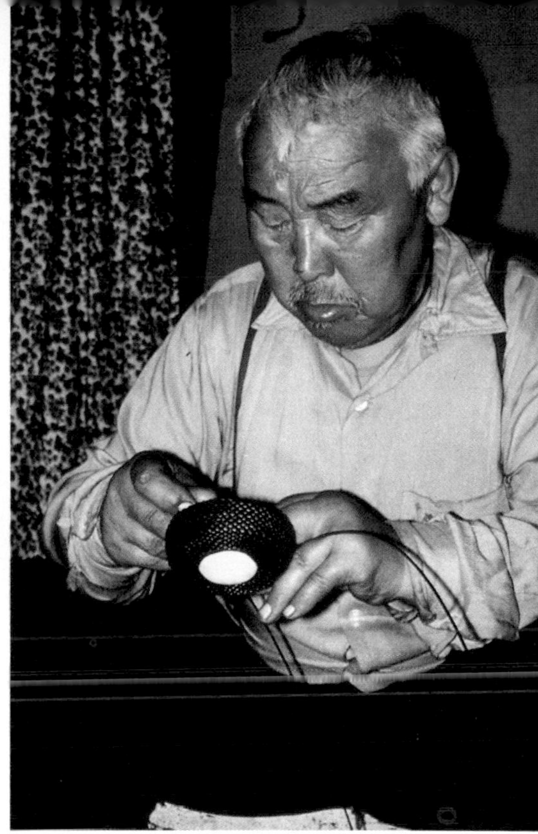

Men weave baskets of baleen (whalebone) and carve animals from ivory. Some still use the ancient bow drill (bottom left). Soapstone (bottom right) has a soft soapy feeling.

N2715R
WIEN ALASKA

MODERN LIFE

Life is somewhat different for Inuit and Yupiks today. Although they still depend on the land and animals for their way of life, there have been many changes.

Hospitals, schools, airstrips, and stores provide for many of their needs. Modern houses have taken the place of sod houses and igloos.

Electric lights and stoves do the work of soapstone lamps. In many areas snowmobiles, airplanes, and motorboats have replaced dogsleds, kayaks, and umiaks. Skin clothing is not usually worn. A few of the animals people once hunted are now more rare. It is against the law to hunt them in great numbers.

ski-doo

But progress has created many problems for people and for animals. Highways and pipelines built by oil companies have been changing the countryside and disturbing the animals on which people depend.

The Trans-Alaskan pipeline

Boots called mukluks are still made with a bearded sealskin sole. The style has changed little over the past 1,000 years.

Inuit and Yupiks like modern ways, but they want to hold on to their old ways, too. They are proud of their customs. Many depend on hunting, fishing, trapping, and gathering for their way of life.

After a whale has been killed, people gather (above) to honor the hunters and the spirit of the whale, and share what they have caught. The blanket toss (right) was an old Inuit custom to help hunters find animals.

Native dance is a form of storytelling—told mainly by hand and arm motions. These children (above) have learned the dance of the seal hunt.

At special times everyone comes together to sing, to dance, and to share their legends.

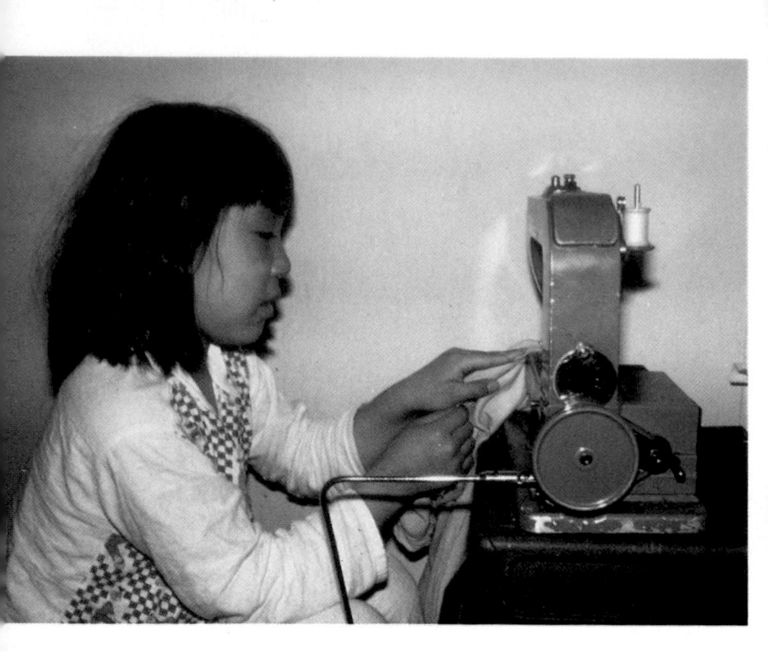

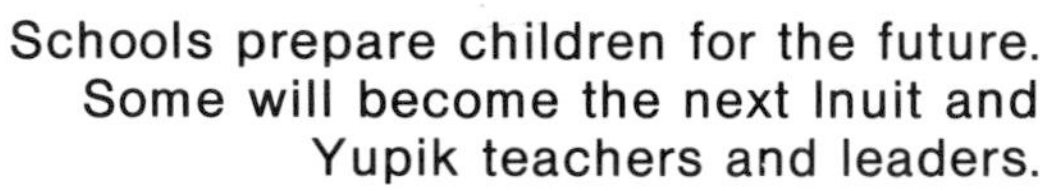

Schools prepare children for the future. Some will become the next Inuit and Yupik teachers and leaders.

Today Inuit and Yupiks use modern tools and modern transportation. Although new industries are being created to provide jobs for people in villages, living off the land continues to be very important to the Inuit and Yupik way of life.

WORDS YOU SHOULD KNOW

afloat(uh • FLOTE)—floating; on the sea

arctic(ARK • tik)—land at the northern tip of the globe, around the north pole

carving(KAR • ving)—cutting away wood, stone, or some other material to make an object of some kind

climate(KLY • mit)—the type of weather in a certain place

coast(KOHST)—land near a shore

custom(KUHS • tum)—a practice common to one group of people

harpoon(har • POON)—a long spear used to catch fish, seals, and whales

husky(HUHSS • kee)—a dog with a heavy coat that lives in the arctic

igloo(IG • loo)—a house made of blocks of snow

industry(IN • dus • tree)—business

inland(IN • land)—away from the sea

Inuit(IN • ooit)—Eskimo people who live from northwestern Alaska, across Canada, into Greenland and speak the Inupiaq language

ivory(EYE • vree)—the material that makes up the tusks of walrus and elephants

kayak(KYE • ak)—a small boat, for one or two people, made of skins stretched over a wooden frame

legend(LEJ • und)—a story that has come down from the past

moss(MAWSS)—a type of tiny plant that grows in moist, swampy places

parka (PAR • kuh) — a fur jacket with a hood, first worn in the arctic

pipeline (PYE • pline) — a long line of pipe for moving liquids or gases

progress (PRAHG • res) — movement toward a better way of life

soapstone (SOHP • stohn) — a soft stone that is easy to carve

sod house (SAHD HAUS) — a house made of sod, or surface soil that is covered with grass and partly underground

subarctic (sub • ARK • tik) — land directly south of the arctic

survive (ser • VYVE) — to continue to live

swamp (SWAHMP) — land that is wet and often covered with water

temperature (TEM • per • uh • cher) — a degree of being hot or cold, as measured on a thermometer

umiak (OO • mee • ak) — a large boat, for ten people or more, made of skins stretched over a wooden frame

waterproof (waht • er • PROOF) — unable to gct wet

Yupik (U • pik) — Eskimo people who live on the western and southwestern coasts of Alaska and speak the Yupik language

INDEX

About the Author

Alice Osinski has had a varied career in the field of education. She has been teacher consultant, director of bicultural curriculum and alternative education programs for Native American children, and producer of educational filmstrips. Ms. Osinski has written several articles about the unique life-style of Native Americans and has coauthored a filmstrip entitled Grandmother White Loon Feather's Thanksgiving. *She has written another book in the New True Book Series entitled* The Sioux.